BEING HEALTHY
Fruit and Vegetables

Heather C. Hudak

Weigl

CALGARY
www.weigl.com

Published by Weigl Educational Publishers Limited
6325 10th Street SE
Calgary, Alberta, Canada
T2H 2Z9

Website: www.weigl.com

Library and Archives Canada Cataloguing in Publication data available upon request.
Fax (403) 233-7769 for the attention of the Publishing Records department.

ISBN 978-1-55388-416-3 (hard cover)
ISBN 978-1-55388-417-0 (soft cover)

Printed in the United States of America
1 2 3 4 5 6 7 8 9 0 12 11 10 09 08

Editor: Heather C. Hudak
Design: Kathryn Livingstone, Terry Paulhus

We gratefully acknowledge the financial support of the Government of Canada
through the Book Publishing Industry Development Program (BPIDP) for our
publishing activities.

Contents

You Are What You Eat 4

Finding Out About
  Fruit and Vegetables 6

From Seed to Serving 8

All About Vegetables 10

Finding Out About Fruit 12

Something for Everyone 14

Are You Being Served? 16

Fitness Fun 18

Time to Dine 20

What Have You Learned? 22

Further Research 23

Glossary/Index 24

You Are What You Eat

From the top of your head to the tip of your toes, you are what you eat. To keep everything working in top form, it is important to eat a balanced diet, drink plenty of water, and be active.

How do you decide what foods to eat? Do you have a special diet, or do you eat whatever you like? There are many guides, such as Canada's Food Guide, that can help you make good choices about the foods you eat.

According to Canada's Food Guide, there are four main food groups. Eating a certain number of servings from each of the food groups every day is one way to help keep your body fit. Healthy eating habits can help prevent heart disease, **obesity**, **diabetes**, and certain types of cancers.

Fruit & Vegetables
5–6 servings

Meat & Alternatives
1–2 servings

Canadian Food Guide
Recommended Daily Servings for Ages 4-13

Milk & Alternatives
2–4 servings

Grain Products
4–6 servings

Food for Thought

Think about the foods you ate today. How do your eating habits compare to those of other people?

Only 50 percent of Canadian children aged 4 to 18 eat the minimum recommended servings of fruit and vegetables each day.

Thirty percent of Canadian children have at least one soft drink each day.

About 75 percent of children in Canada do not eat the recommended number of grain products.

In Canada, nearly 30 percent of children eat French fries at least twice a week.

Finding Out About Fruit and Vegetables

Whether you are chowing down on a crunchy celery stick or biting into a juicy orange, you are likely getting many nutrients you need to keep your body at its best. Eating plenty of fruit and vegetables can help reduce the risk of heart disease and some cancers. Fruit and vegetables can also help prevent eye problems, lower blood pressure, and reduce the risk of stroke.

In North America, fruit and vegetables are readily available at grocery stores and markets in every community. From spinach and carrots to apples and bananas, it is important to eat at least one fruit or vegetable at each meal and to snack on these nutritious treats.

Types of Fruit and Vegetables

Fruit

Vegetables

Leafy Greens

Juice

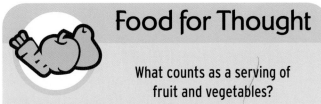

Food for Thought

What counts as a serving of fruit and vegetables?

A serving of raw, frozen, canned, or cooked fruit and vegetables is about 1/2 cup. Fruit juice is equal to about 3/4 cup, while leafy greens require 1 cup.

Most people eat only three servings of fruit and vegetables each day.

From Seed to Serving

Some fruit grows on trees, plants, or vines, while vegetables are often planted in the ground.

Growing Fruit and Vegetables

1 Most fruit and vegetables begin as seeds. Farmers plant the seeds in the ground.

4 Others are dug up from the ground.

2 Next, the farmer waters the seeds so that they will grow into plants.

5 Next, the fruit and vegetables are shipped to stores where you can buy them.

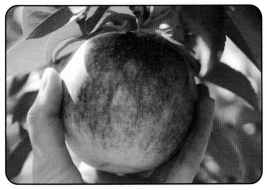

3 When the plant is full grown, it is harvested. Some are plucked from trees that have many fruit.

6 Fruit and vegetables can be eaten raw or cooked as part of a meal.

All About Vegetables

Have you ever helped plant a vegetable garden? Then, you may know that vegetables are the parts of a plant that can be eaten. This includes the stem, root, tuber, flower, bulb, and leaves. Vegetables that come from the bulb may include onions and garlic. Carrots and turnips are root vegetables. Examples of leafy vegetables are kale and spinach, while celery and asparagus are stems. Broccoli and cauliflower come from the flower bud.

The best way to get the most health benefit from vegetables is to eat them steamed, microwaved, or raw. Fewer vitamins and minerals are lost using these methods than stir frying or boiling, for example.

Food for Thought

How can you make sure to get enough vegetables each day?

Fill at least half your plate with vegetables at dinnertime.

Potatoes are a starch, and therefore, do not count toward your daily vegetable count.

Try to eat at least one dark green and one orange vegetable every day. Examples include broccoli, pumpkin, arugula, and squash.

Get the Facts on Nutrition
Learn how to read a food label

When looking for fruit and vegetable products, it is important to read the ingredient list on the food you are buying to check its nutritional value.

The Nutrition Facts table will include the list of **calories** and 13 nutrients.

1

2

3

4

6

Nutrition Facts
Serving Size 1 Cake (43g)
Servings Per Container 5

Amount Per Serving

Calories 200 Calories from Fat 90

	% Daily Value*
Total Fat 10g	**15%**
Saturated Fat 5g	**25%**
Trans Fat 0g	
Cholesterol 0mg	**0%**
Sodium 100mg	**4%**
Total Carbohydrate 26g	**9%**
Dietary Fiber 0g	**0%**
Sugars 19g	
Protein 1g	

Vitamin A 0%	•	Vitamin C 0%
Calcium 0%	•	Iron 2%

* Percent Daily Values are based on a 2,000 calorie diet. Your daily values may be higher or lower depending on your calorie needs:

		Calories:	2,000	2,500
Total Fat	Less than		65g	80g
Sat. Fat	Less than		20g	25g
Cholesterol	Less than		300mg	300mg
Sodium	Less than		2,400mg	2,400mg
Total Carbohydrate			300g	375g
Dietary Fiber			25g	30g

5

1 The facts tell you the serving size and the number of servings in the package. The size of the serving determines the number of calories.

2 Calories tell you how much energy you will get from a serving. Children who get at least one hour of exercise each day should eat between 1,700 and 1,800 calories every day.

3 The first nutrients listed are **fats**. It is important to limit the number of fats you eat each day.

4 The next nutrients listed are fibre, vitamins, and minerals. These are the parts of food that keep your body health and in great shape.

5 The % Daily Value shows how much of the nutrients you need are in one serving of food.

6 The information at the bottom of the label further explains the calorie, nutrient, and % Daily Value information.

Finding Out About Fruit

Have you ever wondered what it would be like to eat a flower? If you have had different types of fruit, then you have tasted many types of flowers. Fruit comes from the ripened **ovaries** of flowering plants. In fact, fruit is the casing that houses a plant's seeds. Some plant ovaries become fleshy, juicy, and sweet fruit. Peaches and mangoes are examples of this type of fruit. Other times, the ovaries form a dry fruit, such as an acorn or chestnut. These dry fruit belong to different food groups.

From the biggest watermelon to the tiniest blueberry, fruit comes in many shapes, sizes, and colours. Red apples, green grapes, yellow bananas, and purple plums are just a few examples of fruit you might eat often.

Food for Thought

Is all fruit edible?

Not all plant ovaries can be eaten as fruit. Some can be poisonous, so it is not a good idea to pluck "fruit" from the flower garden.

Buy canned or frozen fruit that are packed in juice rather than syrup to avoid extra sugar and calories.

Adding fruit to your cereal is a great way to get one serving first thing in the morning.

Each year, nearly 500 million tonnes of fruit are produced around the world.

Fruit and Vegetable Products

Your body needs a certain amount of fats, **carbohydrates**, and **protein** to keep it powered. It is important to find the right balance. If a person eats 1,800 calories each day, about 203 to 293 grams should come from carbohydrates, 40 to 70 grams from fats, and 60 to 158 grams from protein. This chart shows the calories, carbohydrate, fat, and protein content of some basic foods.

Product	Alternative
Grapefruit juice, concentrate 101 calories, 0 gram fat, 24 grams carbohydrates, 1 gram protein	**Grapefruit juice** 96 calories, 0 gram fat, 23 carbohydrates, 1 gram protein
Cooked spinach 34 calories, 1 gram fat, 5 grams carbohydrates, 4 grams protein	**Raw spinach** 7 calories, 0 gram fat, 1 gram carbohydrates, 1 gram protein
Candied fruit 322 calories, 0 gram fat, 83 grams carbohydrates, 0 gram protein	**Kiwi fruit** 61 calories, 1 gram fat, 15 grams carbohydrates, 1 gram protein
Sweet potato, canned, syrup 203 calories, 0 gram fat, 48 grams carbohydrates, 2 grams protein	**Sweet potato, baked with skin** 180 calories, 0 grams fat, 41 grams carbohydrates, 4 grams protein

Did you know that tomatoes, cucumbers, pumpkins, and eggplants are fruit?

Something for Everyone

Chockful of goodness, with few calories and low fat, fruit and vegetables are filled with vitamins and nutrients that can keep your body in top form. In fact, with so many different types of fruit and vegetables, there is something for almost every part of your body.

Some studies have shown that the more fruit and vegetables people eat each day, the less likely they are to suffer from heart disease. Other studies have shown that eating fruit and vegetables can help prevent eye diseases, such as **cataracts**. In addition, eating vitamin A-rich carrots helps keep your vision sharp at night.

What Nutrients do Fruit and Vegetables Have?

Learn how your body uses Fruit and Vegetables

Whole or cut up fruit and vegetables have **dietary fibre**. This helps keep the digestive system working well and reduces blood **cholesterol**. Fruit and vegetables also have **complex carbohydrates** that give your body the energy it needs to get up and go. Potassium, found in some fruit, such as prunes and bananas, helps keep blood pressure low. Vitamin C-rich fruit and vegetables help prevent **scurvy**, maintain tissues, heal cuts, and keep gums healthy. Folic acid helps keep up the red blood cell count in your body.

Gums

Tissues

Digestive System

Are You Being Served?

Eating the right foods and enough of them each day will help you get the vitamins and nutrients you need to stay in great shape. Children ages 4 to 13 should have 5 to 6 servings of fruit and vegetables daily.

Try making a whole grain pita pizza and topping it with your favourite fruit and vegetables, such as pineapple, mushrooms, tomatoes, and peppers.

Try using this chart to plan a daily serving of fruit and vegetables. Then, mix and match items to prepare your fruit and vegetable servings for one week.

zucchini
(125 mL)

spinach
(250 mL)

½ grapefruit

green pepper
(125 mL)

3 apricots

Counting Servings in a Meal

Check out the servings in a meal with fresh bread, chicken, vegetables, a glass of milk, and an orange for dessert.

250 mL (1 cup) vegetables ➤	**2 Fruit & Vegetables** Food Guide Servings
125 mL chicken breast ➤	**1 Meat & Alternatives** Food Guide Servings
1 slice rye bread ➤	**1 Grain Products** Food Guide Servings
250 mL 1% milk ➤	**1 Milk & Alternatives** Food Guide Servings
1 orange ➤	**1 Fruit & Vegetables** Food Guide Servings

sweet potato
(125 mL)

fruit juice
(125 mL)

carrots
(125b mL)

20 grapes

1 large kiwi

Fitness Fun

Healthy eating is just part of keeping your body in top form. In Canada, more than 50 percent of boys and 60 percent of girls do not get enough physical activity. From walking to playing team sports or riding a bike, there are many ways to get the physical activity you need each day.

It is recommended that children take part in at least 90 minutes of physical activity each day. This may include playing a sport, walking a dog, or practising yoga.

Food and Fitness Facts

 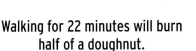 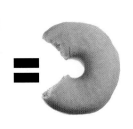

Walking for 22 minutes will burn
half of a doughnut.

Thirty minutes of climbing stairs burns a
small serving of French fries.

Spending 13 minutes on a bike burns
off a glass of pop.

It takes 18 minutes of gardening to
burn off 25 peanuts.

WORK ON THIS

If you ate a doughnut, fries, and a pop today, how
much would you have to work out to burn off
those calories so that you did not gain weight?

Answer: 65 minutes

Calories and Consumption

Your body needs energy to operate. Food provides this energy. A calorie is a unit of energy. Calories
are used to measure the amount of potential energy foods have if they are used by your body. A
gram of carbohydrates or protein has 4 calories, while a gram of fat contains 9 calories. Your body
needs a certain amount of calories each day to function well. If you eat fewer calories than your
body requires, you may lose weight. If you eat more calories, you may gain weight. To maintain
your weight, you need to burn as many calories as you eat. To burn calories, you need to do
physical activity.

Time to Dine

Fresh Fruit Kabobs

What you will need

1 apple
1 banana
1 seedless orange
1/3 cup seedless
  grapes

2/3 cup pineapple
  chunks
1 cup low-fat yogurt
¼ cup shredded
  coconut

Knife
Wooden skewers
2 plates

What to do

1. Begin by washing or peeling the fruit and, with an adult's help, cutting it into bite-size chunks.
2. Place pieces of fruit onto each of the skewers in any combination you like.
3. Spread yogurt on one plate, and roll the skewer in the yogurt.
4. Pour the coconut on the second plate, and roll the yogurt-covered skewer in coconut.

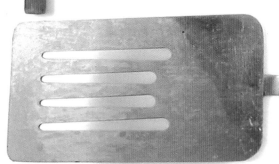

Scrumptious Salad

What you will need

2 mandarin oranges

1 cup of sliced strawberries

4 ounces of soy blue cheese crumble

A handful of cashews

3 tablespoons of red wine vinegar and orange juice

1 ½ tablespoons canola oil

1/4 teaspoon dry mustard

1/3 teaspoon poppy seeds

Knife

Two mixing bowls

Wooden spoon

What to do

1. Tear up the spinach into bite-size pieces, and place in one of the mixing bowls.
2. Peel the oranges and divide them into pieces. Put them in the bowl with the spinach. Add strawberries.
3. Mix the red wine vinegar, orange juice, canola oil, dry mustard, and poppy seeds in the other mixing bowl. This will be the salad dressing.
4. Pour the dressing over the salad. Place 2 cups of salad on a plate, and sprinkle with blue cheese and cashews.

What Have You Learned?

What is fruit?

Answer: the casing that houses a plant's seeds

What are vegetables?

Answer: the parts of a plant that can be eaten

What are the four food groups?

Answer: Fruit and Vegetables Milk and Alternatives Meat and Alternatives Grain Products

What are vitamin-A rich carrots good for?

Answer: keeping your vision sharp at night

How can you burn off half of a doughnut?

Answer: walk for 22 minutes

What is potassium good for?

Answer: keeping blood pressure low

Further Research

How can I find out more about fruit, vegetables, and healthy eating?

Most libraries have computers that connect to a database that contains information on books and articles about different subjects. You can input a key word and find material on that person, place, or thing you want to learn more about. The computer will provide you with a list of books in the library that contain information on the subject you searched for. Non-fiction books are arranged numerically, using their call number. Fiction books are organized alphabetically by the author's last name.

Websites

For a copy of Canada's Food Guide, surf to **www.hc-sc.gc.ca/fn-an/food-guide-aliment/index-eng.php**.

To learn more about healthy living, download the guide at **www.healthycanadians.gc.ca/pa-ap/cg-cg_e.html**.

For information about your body, fitness, food and other health topics, visit **http://kidshealth.org/kid**.

Glossary

calories: units of measure for the amount of heat made by a food when it is used by the body

carbohydrates: a compound made of carbon, hydrogen, and oxygen; sugars and starches

cataracts: transparent covers around the lens of the eye that block the passage of light

cholesterol: a type of fat produced in the body and also found in some foods. Cholesterol is used by the body to make hormones and build cell walls

complex carbohydrates: nutritionally dense compounds that are rich in vitamins, minerals, and fiber

diabetes: a disease in which the body has too much blood sugar; treated with insulin, a substance that controls the use of sugar by the body

dietary fibre: part of the plant cell that does not digest and helps maintain a healthy digestive system

fats: animal tissue consisting chiefly of cells containing much greasy or oily matter

obesity: being excessively overweight

ovaries: the part of a flower that contains the seeds and grows into a fruit

protein: a substance that is needed by all living things

scurvy: a disease caused by not having enough vitamin C in the diet

Index

bulb 10

calories 11, 12, 14, 19
Canada's Food Guide 4, 5, 23
carbohydrates 15, 19
cholesterol 15

fibre 11, 15
fitness 18, 19, 23
flower 10, 12

heart disease 4, 6, 14

leaves 10

potassium 15, 22

root 10

seeds 9, 12, 21, 22
stem 10

tuber 10